Holding the Body Back

Poems by
Marsha Witham Whitman

1ST WORLD PUBLISHING

1ST WORLD
PUBLISHING

SAN FRANCISCO ❖ FAIRFIELD ❖ DELHI

Holding the Body Back

1st World Publishing
PO Box 2211
Fairfield, IA 52556
www.1stworldpublishing.com

Book & Cover Photo & Design
Melanie Gendron
melaniegendron999@gmail.com

Cover Photo
The cover is a picture of the author's mother in 1940 at around age 19. Photographer unknown.

Author Photo
Frank Whitman

First Edition

Library of Congress Cataloging-in-Publication Data

ISBN: 978-1-4218-3649-2

For Frank.

Table of Contents

Part 1 — Family Matters

Part 2 — Why I Don't Eat Duck

Part 1 — FAMILY MATTERS

Hubbard, Iowa 1926

The Iowa great-aunts congregate
on the steps of the white clapboard Church,
weighty bodies in printed shirtwaists and sturdy shoes,
gray, waved hair tucked under cloche hats.

Great Grandma Anna Hedlund's house
is an easy trip in a Model T, down Main Street,
closed and shuttered for the Sabbath.

Sunday dinner is roast pork, corn pudding,
mashed potatoes on the ironstone Tea Leaf,
hot rolls and a sweet fruit compote.

Each course is served up with Bible talk,
gossip from Grandpa RR's drugstore,
whispered tête-à-têtes among the women
about the latest family matters.

After dessert the men smoke, the women do needlework,
the youngest cousins throw balls in the shady yard.

The afternoon slips behind the oaks in dappled light.
The older uncles grow quiet, nod off,
but the great-aunts stand vigil, brows furrowed,
sensing the intrusion of a future branch of the family
eavesdropping through the decaying leaves
of their photo album.

Missouri Connection

From the Aux Vases front stoop,
she gazes out of the Daguerreotype,
exactly my face shape, square jaw,
prominent bones, teeth slightly clenched,
and I feel the tightness of her stiff,
starched collar around my neck.
Moments earlier she had twisted her hair just so,
my great, great aunt, and smoothed the loose
strands around her ears, perhaps also pinched
her cheeks and bit her lips for color.
In long-sleeved, full-skirted dress
she sits with her sisters, all models of
modesty and Christian fortitude,
in heat and humidity, perfectly, painfully still,
but across a century I sense the body at work,
pulsing red of veins, blue passion of eyes,
invisible spasms of the future quivering.

Ancestor Worship

Far from any road we might have traveled,
this tranquil half acre in northern California
along Cemetery Road
is all that's left of Piccard,
abandoned when the railroad
terminated at Dorris,
leaving no one to tend the farms,
only gentle hills of live oaks
and Western Junipers
interspersed with fists of wildflowers.

Govan High and Mary Jane Lincoln,
my great, great grandparents are here
on a knoll, under a bountiful tree,
beyond a border of dry grasses
above a field as green as emeralds.

It is silent except for a mockingbird
and the hum of distant irrigation pipes.

Over the low hills of the Butte Valley,
on the distant horizon,
Mount Shasta preens in the sun,
capped by a plume of luminous cloud.

Half Past Eight

Officer Club dances on Saturday night,
a babysitter and fish sticks for dinner.
Dad in dress uniform at the piano,
smelling of Old Spice, a Pall Mall
clasped in the side of his mouth,
wisp of smoke making his eyes squint.
"I'll be down to get you in a taxi, Honey!"
Mother upstairs curling her eyelashes,
dressing table a clutter of powder,
lipsticks, and bobby pins;
stockings, slips, and indecisions
strewn across the bed.
"Now, dearie, don't be late…"
She descends the stairs
in a whisper of Arpège,
swish of red taffeta,
a wreath of rhinestones.
He looks at his watch.
"I want to be there
when the band starts playing."
We jockey for position,
press our faces to the window,
watch as our movie-star parents
disappear into the glamourous dark.

Learning to be the Light

In the weeks after school was out,
in the years before life got complicated,
Vacation Bible School offered
pleasant days of paper bag lunches,
Hawaiian Punch, and no air-conditioning.

With friends named Mary, Linda, and Sally,
we memorized verses, competed at Bible drills,
sang, "This Little Light of mine,"
"Give me oil in my lamp,"
"Jesus wants me for a sunbeam."

During craft time, with our crayons,
blunt scissors, colored paper,
we pasted collages and learned about Jesus —
how he fed the five thousand,
how he healed the blind, the lame, the leper,
how he loves all the little children of the world.

Trinity Baptist — San Antonio, 1959

Hymns float in the dusky air in four-part harmony.
The blue Texas sky fades beneath a halo of light.
Softly and tenderly Jesus is calling.

The air rustles with praise and confession.
Sunday evening wraps its arms around us.
Sweet hour of prayer.

Cicadas ring out along the fringes of the silence.
Stars gather together for their celestial ride.
Father, we thank thee for the night.

The service gently concludes in benediction.
Voices crescendo in choral amens.
Wherever He leads, I'll go.

Our Chevy hums as it traverses the miles.
Bluebonnets hide in the dark hills.
Open my eyes that I may see.

Prayers are the last words of the night.
Faith sings gently through my dreams.
Jesus loves me, this I know.

Secondhand Smoke

A workman, tobacco smoke,
and a tumble back five decades,
where cigarettes make gray halos
and pulsing orange points like fireflies
against the sultry Georgia night,
as heat lightning and thunder murmur
beyond the cool stone of the front porch.

Smoking pretend cigarettes,
cousins whisper and giggle,
each voice its own music,
rising and falling, underscored
by crickets and highway traffic.

Adults, cool in cotton shorts,
lounge on white iron chairs
or lean against the bannister,
red packs of unfiltered Pall Malls
in hand or pocket, the women
daintily picking thin flakes
of tobacco off their tongues,
the men, cigarettes dangling,
talking business, arguing politics
as puff by puff, the fiery tips
curl and devour the paper.

Last years —Yolo County, CA

Crippled by arthritis, Grandma Witham
lived for fifteen years in the
upholstered chair by the window
watching strips of shadow
move across the worn Bible on her lap.
At first, she read or murmured
the memorized verses,
but later the cortisone senility
began to box in her brain, and her eyes,
milky blue like marbles, searched warily,
like an animal entering a new place.

In the deep recesses of her cerebral cage,
what was she thinking all those years?
Did fragments of the past flit in and out
and familiar faces tease her,
like food just out of reach?
Or did eighty years smear together
with the reassuring smells of cows,
cooking, soap powder, and urine,
leaving her disassembled mind
as curled and comfortable as sleep?

Stage Mother

Mother loved the Show Bus
that took her from suburbia to Broadway
to catch the Wednesday matinee —
Hello Dolly, Gypsy, Annie Get Your Gun,
and about a hundred others —
memorialized in stacks of Playbills.

I never heard her say a negative word
about even the most dismal flop.

When we showed talent and interest,
Mother read *Variety*, clipping the auditions,
kept abreast of local productions,
knew all the stories of hometown girls
who made it big.

Mother said she wanted to be
"the Grandma Moses of the stage,"
though she never took an audition,
memorized a line, or even read a play,
content to immerse herself in the costumes,
music, and glamor from her seat in the audience,
living her dream below the footlights.

German and Other Lessons — 1975

I am exuberant at twenty-five as I bound off the bus
across from Central Park at 96th and 5th.
Beyond the awning, the doorman, the marble foyer,
the tiny elevator, all velvet and mirrors,
is shabby from decades of up and down.

On the 9th floor, a small, stale anteroom,
a darkly furnished corridor,
a parlor where heavy, ornate chairs
crowd the library of leather-bound books
and old encyclopedias, filled with misinformation.
From the tall window in the washroom,
light stripes the room like a Dutch painting,
and she, in her wheelchair, waiting,
in black, always with a thin aura of mourning.

Earl Grey scents the hours of our discussions:
Schnitzler, Rilke, Hoffmansthal.
German lieder, psychoanalysis.
Vienna before the war.

Her thin, white hair is gathered in a bun,
but escaped wisps frame her face,
an eight-decade etching of intellect, love, loss.
She says it is always a shock to catch one's reflection
in the mirror and momentarily wonder
who the old woman is.

Middle Sisters

I loved you, sister, despite
your blonde beauty-pageant looks,
perfect organizational skills,
set against my misbehaving curls,
Chubbies from Sears Roebuck,
a tendency towards messiness.

I loved you, sister, though the boys
liked you best, and friends invited you over,
while I practiced piano or watched
Million Dollar Movie at four o'clock.

I loved you, sister, although
you eloped at twenty,
had the first grandson, moved to California,
while I trod the traditional route
of settling down close to our parents.

But I think I loved you most, sister,
when you called that December morning
of 1978 to say you'd had a baby girl.

Four years ago to the day,
I was told by doctors in the know
that I would probably
have no children.

But now I could tell you,
in August I would give your girl a cousin.
We had something in common then —
the child just leaving your body;
the new life beginning in mine.

Sunbeam Mixmaster

In the Vermeer light of her Georgia kitchen,
over her chrome-edged, white enamel table,
Grandma gathered her essentials:
Gold Medal flour, Domino sugar, Morton's salt,
snowy mounds of promise.

Amidst a gaggle of eggs, butter, milk,
glass and metal jumble
of bowls, cups, and spoons,
the Sunbeam Mixmaster's black and white body
strutted with its stylish rooster-comb handle,
miraculous silver beaters in lieu of claws.

Grandma was a wizard with her Sunbeam.
The aroma of chocolate chip cookies,
gingerbread, cinnamon swirls baking,
can still bring her back into a room.

Dichotomy

He is very handsome still
with his uneven smile.
His laugh divides his face
into a hundred tiny lines.
I want to trace them with my finger.
His voice sounds as it always does
as he tries to cross the silence,
but the past is still crippling,
and words limp between us.

In mean remarks he makes her aware
that her beauty has begun to fade,
leaving her early in the morning
in her shapeless housecoat and pearls.
I stay home from school
so I can hear her singing
as she does the dishes,
folds the laundry, dusts
around the house,
her throaty alto mourning
about "Blues in the Night"
or "A Good Man is Hard to Find."

Family Recipes

My grandmother scribbled notes
alongside the recipes of her
spattered cookbook pages,
penciling in by Parker House rolls,
ginger snaps, raised doughnuts:
not so much flour,
bake 15 minutes longer,
my mother's favorite.

I am perpetually jotting down poems
like fragments of my life,
so those feelings might not be forgotten.

I am trying to remember,
or figure out,
how to do it better.

Mother Love

Her fervent good-night kisses bore into me.
I tell her it hurts, but she does it anyway —
punishing me for pushing her
out of my body.
The years reach monstrously between us,
while I am the ogre who urges her to grow.

Naked, out of the shower,
the water drips off my nipples,
like the thin bluish fluid
that nourished her once,
and my abdomen still bears
the outward reminders
that in creating her,
I stretched my own boundaries.

Nature Center — Cusp of Spring

Our first hike of the season —
the woods are cool; rotted leaves
make soft mud under our feet.

With hands in pockets,
in matching jackets of red, green, blue,
two little dark heads race around me,
flanked by dry undergrowth
and bare, familiar trees.
Their chatter disturbs the late winter.

Around the pond, the ground
is swollen with impending life,
but no movement yet.

At the edge of the trail,
the old apple orchard welcomes us
with gnarled arms.
Our shadows seem at home here
in any season's sunlight.

I sit on a dead log, hollowed out.
The children swing on branches
or roll in the prickly, yellow grass.
A tiny woodpecker keeps busy,
unafraid of our intrusion.
Two robins hop out of the brush.
The air is good —
sweet and saturated with promise.

Until We Meet Again

The dollies are laid out to be bathed,
dressed up with best clothes, bonnets and shoes,
like children readied to travel.

I, their grandmother, wash, dry, and iron
their other dresses, fold and stack them
as neatly as trousseau linens.

12-year-old Charlotte ties name tags on their wrists:
Huggums, Sharon, Emily, Molly,
Lena, Violetta, Monica, Sara,
and groups them for a farewell photo.

Together, we lay them gently in a plastic box,
seal the lid, tearfully say good-bye,
and send them off to storage
for their silent journey
to the next generation.

Holding the Body Back

The young girl's breasts,
as her towel slips for a moment,
are streaked like mine were
with signs of growth —
rose-colored lines
holding the body back.

And though, with time,
they fade from pink to beige,
they never wholly disappear,

like things you'd rather not remember —
those incurable hidden bruises
that ache inside
when something jogs the memory
and presses up against them.

Older Sister

Your face never changes.
The lamp light is on it now
as you lounge on the sofa,
gently biting your tongue, as the plot
intensifies in your romance novel,
lords, ladies, and castles keeping you
lost in another time and place.

I sit in a straight chair by the fire,
a book of essays about psychoanalysis
and art pressing on my lap,
but I am more engrossed in your face.

I can imagine us old in this house,
children grown and gone,
diminishing eyesight, graying hair,
bodies growing brittle.

Maybe after days of quiet,
we'll have music and conversation,
reminiscing over family photo albums,
rehashing old arguments.

But maybe you'll read your novels,
and I'll read my essays
and remark to myself
how your face never changes.

Hiking Twilight Park — Late 1980s

When Granddad was in his sixties,
they camped in the Sierras.
Dad said there was sheer rock,
and Granddad climbed it like a boy.
He told me this as we walked the mountain,
resting after a steep incline.

"He wanted to live to be a hundred.
Someone should have done something more.
I should have done something more.
He was in there after the stroke.
He squeezed my hand."

The woods are cool and Dad strides ahead
with his distinctive walk,
over rocks, water pipes, fallen branches.
In his sixties he is healthy too,
only burdened by the missteps
of his daughters.

The years are rushing over the precipice
like water over Santa Cruz Falls,
and the words that want to be said
stay hidden behind hurt feelings
of the past.
At least my son has his name —
my gift to him.

College Bound

Our moment of separation
is so loaded with emotion,
so bloated with words unsaid
that it's a relief when it's over,
and we split off in our own directions.

Each good-bye moves us
one step closer to that final one.

I would like
to have held your hand,
or had you hold mine.

We hide our eyes
behind dark glasses,
and say lightheartedly,
have a good trip,
I love you.

We are so very brave.

Empty Nesters

Anxious about our son, we reflect
on the mottled, bony sycamore, recently stripped
by the wolf pack winds that howl down
from across the Canadian tundra,
which disperse the giant leaves —
dried up, edges curled,
washed out remnants of themselves.
The sky bundles up in rain-heavy clouds,
billowing shoulders hiding the light,
chilling us until we turn the heat up,
glad the living room is painted sunshine yellow.
We feel like hostages inside the grey walls of November
and know that in the colorful eighty degrees
of Los Angeles autumn,
our son is not anxious about us.

Strangers in the Mirror

Over her Irish coffee, her eyes are enormous
behind sad glasses, as we study each other.
Our faces, with slightly too much make-up,
still contain a remnant of beauty,
despite decades of emotion
around the mouth, across the cheeks.

We try to remember the moment
when men stopped looking at us,
when we became invisible.
Youth just packed its bags one morning
and left us staring at strangers in the mirror.

Whoever thought it would be this hard?
Whoever thought this fragile folding
of ivory skin could feel so tragic?

Heartthrob

Mother talks in her morphine sleep,
as her tube-nourished body diminishes.
I follow her voice as her mind
flits from one year to the next,
free to wander the past.
I sit and listen to the
monitor that sings her heart —
the soundtrack to the liquid confines
of my just beginning,
the familiar, comforting
pulse of home.

Water Damage

The washer hose burst,
the downstairs flooded,
and water seeped out the garage door,

after saturating every room, every closet,
leaving shoes like boots of blue fur,
soaked books and papers,
wet smell, mold smell.

Workmen filled the dumpster
with soggy debris,
while Dad, mostly focused forward,
cared only about a missing old Homberg
and a genuine gold piece he had collected.

Years later, cleaning out his houses,
we realized home movies were missing —
we sisters building snowmen in Arlington,
climbing haystacks at Grand-dad's Yolo farm,
running on the beach at St. Simons,
singing "Heart of my Heart" on a summer night
on the back stoop in Montgomery.

But the wet reels filled with family history
unraveled from their flimsy cans and drowned
when that hose burst,
leaving us to mourn, late after the fact,
this ticket back to our childhood.

Good-bye Before Hello

Tiny life that never was
anything but heartbeat and love,
ungendered, incomplete,
an excitement, an energy,
and now a mourning.

Little unnamed life that let go
of the viscous black and
life-giving waves
of your mother's womb,
insufficient for keeping or burial.

Child of my child.
Loved, though never known.

Yard Goods

The grass is a bolt of green velvet
embroidered with blue hyacinths.

Time to weed out the winter clothes,
season after season, barely worn,
hoping they'll fit next year,
hoping they'll come back in style.

Mother's blouses and dresses,
crammed at the back of the closet,
have lost her scent
and can finally be relinquished,
the cloth still strong and useful,
even now at the decade mark.

My tendons, as the doctor explained,
are more like worn fabric,
with thin and weakened threads,
no easy seams to sew.

Time tries to unravel me —
and repairs leave a texture
that always chafes a little
on the side closest to the heart.

New Owner

Fifty-one stumps are squatting amidst
the scattered mounds of wood chips
and skulking yellow machines.
In one afternoon, they demolished
the unhurried decades
of those tall green patriarchs
who watched our children grow.

The collapsed red barn is down too,
making way for four new houses
with pristine gravel walks,
and perfect gardens.

No more tangled dance of old leaves
whipped across the rocky field
nor the twists and random turns of twigs
sketched untidily on the changeable sky.
No more rabbits burrowing under
the brush pile where the wild mint spread,
or the red fox grooming in the spotlight
of a fragile, familiar moon.

Greatness Passing

His voice, which once commanded squadrons,
has released its last sound.
The house holds its breath too,
as though waiting for bells to toll.

No officers come to ease this hero
out the door, just the undertaker
and two women on the a.m. shift,
awkward with his weight.

 No flag-draped coffin or black hearse,
 just a discreet blue van
to carry him from home one last time.
We stand in our robes and slippers,
wave at his cortege from the front steps,
aware of governments crumbling.

White Pine

In 1917 Silvermine was hemp farms
and working mills strung at intervals
on the falls along the river.

Our White Pine was a sapling
in a stand of siblings — scrawny wisps
of green needle clusters, lightly powdered
by the dust of carts beyond stone walls.

Under gales and torrents,
hurricanes named Donna, Gloria, Sandy,
weighty snow of yearly blizzards,
our white pine flourished,
grew with its brothers, towering over
the slow changes of the passing years:
farms into neighborhoods,
carts into automobiles,
dirt into asphalt.

Lightning found this sentinel at our back gate,
creating a wound that welcomed wood ants,
weakening its core with a zigzag of golden dust,
and on a day of blue sky and first forsythia,
a single unexpected gust of March air
delivered the death blow —
one final moan, a shutter, and it crashed down,
leaving behind a stump with a hundred rings.

Winter Vignette

In the cold air against the barn,
snowflakes are shadows
which barely caress my face
as they float to the ground.

My footfalls disappear in the quiet,
and time seems to dissipate,
as though tomorrow is on hold,
and grief will not be necessary.

The edges of the yard fray into darkness,
but the path and the railing are faintly illuminated,
as though someone is lighting candles
behind diaphanous clouds.

Selling our Parents' House — Memorabilia I

We empty the attic, the closets,
footlockers and cedar chests,
let the husbands do the heavy lifting.

The air carries a slight musty smell
as we start to sort through 97 years.

Photo albums, school programs,
playbills, Broadway tickets, invitations,
letters, tissue thin newspaper clippings,
bundled Holiday cards, inaccurate maps,
souvenir books of matches, travel brochures,
diaries and calendars.

The years and decades are a jumbled chronology,
paraphernalia tossed willy-nilly into untidy drawers,
questions like missing puzzle pieces.

The hungry dumpster is waiting outside the house,
eager to devour the past.

Selling our Parents' Home — Memorabilia II

Four sisters convene at the house
for a week in February,
let each rope of sadness
braid with the others into a lifeline
as we empty things out,
rehash our lives, keep an ear out
for our parents' voices.

Our eldest melancholy sister,
burdened with good intentions,
sits in a corner of her old bedroom,
crying over boxes of papers,
each card and letter a reminder
of something she should have done.

Number two, meticulous and energetic,
is impatient with her past,
only able to bear a cursory look,
as she lets most of the decades go,
nipping outdoors for a cigarette,
before taking on more practical,
emotionally unencumbered things.

I am the archivist sister,
predisposed to hoard the past
and load myself with the most boxes to sort,
anxious to salvage our family history.

Our youngest sister, despite
lingering fatigue from chemotherapy,
makes us laugh, keeps our spirits up,
twirling in and out of our rooms
modeling Mamie Eisenhower hats
on her white, half- inch hair.

Visiting California in March

After the parched monochrome months
of Connecticut winter, he takes us
to the Santa Monica Farmers' Market,
with its jumble of white canopied stalls —
oranges, avocados, eggplants —
filling our color-starved eyes
with the flowers and fresh produce
of Southern California.

Behind its marine-layer mask,
the sun gently pulses,
as he fills his basket with strawberries,
sunchokes, asparagus, potatoes,
and Santa Barbara Sea bass —
the last of the season.

We taste sweet dates and almonds,
and admire the artichokes
cuddling their hidden hearts,
as he sniffs lemons for his Beurre Blanc.

We converse carefully around the memories,
across the minefield of growing up and apart,
finding it safer to confine the conversation
to the exuberant plenty of his life in California,
and the boundless possibilities of the next meal.

Moira for the Weekend

She packs up the important things:
two dolls, her pink blanket,
play clothes, one fancy dress.
She knows her air mattress
under the skylights in the green room
is waiting, scattered with stuffed animals
and Little Golden Books —
remnants of her mother's childhood.

We play dress up with scarves,
munch leftover Halloween candy,
fold, glue, and decorate a paper Christmas village,
visit the Maritime Center, eat fish and chips
by the white swans and winterized boats
of Long Island Sound.

We spend the evening with Mary Poppins,
march across the roofs of Victorian London,
slide up the banister, have tea on the ceiling
laughing with Uncle Albert.

At seven, she is tall and slender,
seemingly boneless as she sings
and dances with the chimney sweeps,
joyously twirling and leaping,
her gap-toothed jack-o-lantern smile
lighting up the room.

Birthday Blizzard — February 9

The wind paints snowlines across the window,
sculpts shapes on the skylights, whistles and sings
as it binds the doors and driveway.

Three miles down the road, at Riverside Cemetery,
rolling hills of white cuddle with bands of evergreen.

I'm wondering if there are just ashes in urns
and frozen bodies there, beneath the mounds of snow,
names and dates on stones, barely remembered.

Or, like in *Our Town* and *Spoon River Anthology*,
do the spirits come out on a regular basis,
oblivious of the temperature, to reminisce
about the treacherous weather and the slippery years?

Kindly Light

Around the den under the lamps
that were Mother and Dad's,
decorative boxes are arranged
in awkward towers —
rounds, rectangles, hearts —
each shape stuffed with decades
of family photos.

I always plan to reorganize them,
to send some to my sisters,
put some into albums,
let some go.

But month after month, the stacks
stay put, occasionally dusted,
rarely rearranged.

I am comforted by the contents
of these cardboard domiciles —
captured moments with the faces,
"which I have loved long since
and lost awhile."

Tuesdays with Paige

She pulls herself up by the crib slats
as she sees me peeking around the door.
She bounces up and down,
her mouth an oval of delight.

Her inflected babble begins
as I lift her out, set her down,
unsteady, bowlegged, arms akimbo
until she takes the lead,
using her walker like a miniature old lady.

Stacking blocks, colorful books,
baby dolls get equal attention,
even a half-full plastic bottle,
which makes a crinkly sound as she squeezes.

Edith, the kitty, saunters across the room.
"Cat," Paige announces, then looks around
at stuffed dogs, bunnies, elephants.
"Cat," she concludes.

She studies my eyes, nose, and teeth,
examines jewelry, explores watches,
pushes the buttons on her busy box,
moves in happy abandon to the tinny music.

Pebble Beach House — Mid-November

His shoes are lined up neatly by the bed.
His shirts, meticulously ironed,
hang in the closet all facing the same way,
his rolled socks and folded underwear
layered in drawers.

Pictures of family members, past and present,
crowd the tables in every room.
A large print hymn book lies open on the Baldwin.

The orchids, birds of paradise, and prayer plants,
watered weekly by the housekeeper,
are still thriving, but the clocks, unwound,
stare with passive faces.

In the yard, the silhouette of a crow
perches on a spar left for the woodpeckers.
An early hummingbird, like a tiny angel,
flashes by the window en route to the bottle brush.

I think I hear Dad moving about the kitchen,
stirring Equal into his mug of black coffee,
slowly shuffling down the hall.
He'll light the gas fire, sit in his favorite chair,
read his Bible, then call his children on the East Coast,
as he watches the pines of Del Monte Forest
emerge against his beloved western sky.

After Deciding to Sell the Pebble Beach House

The suitcases sit sadly by the door.
Dad's letters, papers, photos all boxed up.
Our family doesn't live here anymore.

Goodwill donations pile up on the floor,
the drawers and closets clean and empty now.
The suitcases wait sadly by the door.

The sandpipers still race along the shore.
The otters and the cormorants won't know
our family doesn't live here anymore.

Each sister chooses jewelry mother wore.
Some rooms still wear the wallpaper she chose.
The suitcases wait sadly by the door.

Our last good-bye takes longer than before.
The suitcases wait sadly by the door.
Our family doesn't live here anymore.

Agnus in Decline

Agnus, our old Bichon Frise,
still greets us with a wagging tail.
Twice daily insulin shots,
loss of sight and loss of hearing,
have not managed to fully erode
her puppy-like ways.

I treat her with hospice care:
let her eat what she likes,
keep her comfortable,
hope I'll know when to let her go.

On a warm June evening, on our deck,
a bird is singing its twilight song.
The yard is wreathed in pink mountain laurel,
raspberry-colored peonies, yellow foxgloves.

Agnus lifts her white, fuzzy head
and sniffs the new summer grass
as we sit pressed closely together,
quietly savoring the remains of the day.

Tuesday's Child

Our baby grandson arrives
rosy, wrinkled, coiled like a fiddle fern,
his miniature fingers and toes,
mouth, eyes, nose
perfectly formed.

Our daughter cradles her boy,
a modern Madonna in a shaft of light.

It is a May morning,
irises at their peak.
Deep purple fleur-de-lis,
and cherub clouds bounce
across the sky —

this day, so full of grace.

A Life in Idioms

I dodged the bullet,
beat the odds,
caught the cancer in time,
a near miss.

I barked up the wrong tree,
missed the boat,
got caught in the crossfire,
lost my touch.

I didn't sweat the small stuff,
cry over spilt milk,
once in a blue moon
got a second chance.

I sat tight, pitched in,
cut to the chase,
did the right thing,
faced the music.

I put my shoulder to the wheel,
kept my eye on the ball,
jumped on the bandwagon,
am still alive and kicking.

Part 2 — WHY I DON'T EAT DUCK

Why I Don't Eat Duck

I never asked to be around in April
when snow melt and rain
caused our inebriated pond
to stagger above its banks,
nor to see the duck flotilla
diminish day by day, victim of
lurking turtles, or midnight raids
by coyote and fox.

I never asked to find the last feathery ball,
curled and camouflaged in the grasses,
missing half of one tiny webbed foot,
or to feel a need to nourish her,
morning and evening, with bits of bread.

Week by summer week, I watched her grow,
confident it was I who taught her
how to swim, to fly.
From the violent thunder of July
through parched August,
I worried like a mother.

At the first breath of Autumn,
fully fledged, she seemed to sense
the other ducks flying overhead at dusk,
and in late September, without warning,
she simply disappeared and left
an unexpected imprint on my heart.

Connecticut April

From the grey branches,
a rosy hesitancy.
From the pocked umber earth,
an emerald haze.
On the black lattice of the tallest tree,
against the cerulean sky,
one crimson cardinal!
And wildly waving,
the forsythia, the daffodils, the dandelions —
Yellow!
       Yellow!
              Yellow!

Ice Melt

March exhales a warm sigh,
and the choking ice flows
begin to disappear into the river.

In a thin coat and no hat,
I tilt my face upwards
to catch the heat of the stingy sun.

Mergansers with harlequin heads
and glass-bead eyes bobble on the mill pond,
while a swooping black-capped chickadee
sings his descending two note song,

The buttonwood branches
are quivering with their buds-to-be,
and the blood in the waking maples
oozes down to the waiting spigot.

The Northeast winter muscled its way in
with a triple punch of snow, arctic air, and ice,
but even this ruthless season is no match
for the undefeated turning of the year.

Anniversary Tree

Bare viburnum branches
on the tree above the river
tilt towards spring.
Beneath their trunk,
tiny flowers on dark myrtle
appear — blue stars.

For three seasons, I longed for
their green, glossy leaves
and perfect white flower puffs.

Isn't life like that?
Always anticipating
the moments of happiness —
to hold a ball of blossoms in May —
then remembering and waiting
the rest of the year.

Spring Warfare

Brown, mottled sparrows with their striped helmets
monopolize the bird feeder, chatter and fight,
keep a wall of tail feathers up to ward off
titmouse, nuthatch, chickadee.
Even the tiny goldfinch can't get in.

Azaleas fan the flame of Spring
as the birds battle for territory, prepare their nests.
Mourning doves swoop in and out,
with an occasional burst of blackbirds.

Watchful from the silence of the kitchen window,
I hope to catch a glimpse
of red-bellied woodpecker, rose-breasted Grosbeak,
and warily search the roofs and fence post,
for the Cooper's hawk.

Late May Garden

The grape hyacinths, bleeding hearts,
Johnny jump-ups unfold.
From morning to afternoon
they stretch and change
as inevitably as children.

Hostas do their leafy dance,
green fireworks in slow motion,
and blue-flowered myrtle
gather along the garden floor.

April painted the black and white world
with yellow daffodils and forsythia.
Now May expands the palette
in lavender points of iris
pink balls of rhododendron,
and blue clematis creeping over the fence.

Purple Lupines burst from the ground
like torpedoes!

Departure

I liked your philosophies as we tossed hay
and poured oats in the stiff, cracked buckets.
The barn was misty with steaming manure
and the cold morning breath of horses.

In the Spring, you told me earth lore,
as we planted peas and waited for lilacs.
Maytime and *My Delight* whinnied from their stalls
while violets spread in the grass.

When *Star*, your oldest pony, died in the night,
you buried her beyond the vegetable patch,
spending the day readying the earth as though to plant.

You said, "I want to go quick, like that,"
but death only got you half-way,
leaving you a body with useless parts.

In the nursing home, I spooned the pudding
into your mouth, and it dribbled out.
I wiped it, and the tears, because you couldn't.

That last time, I brought you tulips,
and you said, "beautiful," with your twisted mouth,
because Spring was coming.

When I got the card that said you'd died,
I was glad you'd left that body.
It was when the wild asparagus sprouted by old *Star's* grave,
just when the lilacs bloomed.

Dementia Wing

This is the final chapter of an old story,
faces etched like ancient parchment,
bodies bleached and shriveled,
blue script of tired veins
scrolling up arms as brittle as dry leaves.

Their names evoke the past:
Adelaide, the Vaudeville performer,
pencil thin legs dangling from her chair —
a dream of pirouettes in front of velvet curtains;
Edna the socialite, flitting about,
delightfully confused,
thanking everyone for coming;
Horace, the opera singer,
toothless mouth forming words
which his vocal cords betray;
and Victor, the businessman, community pillar,
whose major activity now is rolling his trouser legs
up and down.

They doze, eat, sleep,
these lives left hanging,
unable to wonder
what they're waiting for.

Farewell to Sky

Green spreads like a flood
and begins to cover everything.

Trees surround our yard,
no longer the crossed swords of winter,
but draped with newborn leaves.

The sun splashes down,
squandering itself
in forsythia and daffodils.

I begin to miss the limitless sky
with its blue embrace.
I know what it feels like
to have the bare bones of your life
weighed down by passing seasons.

I find myself looking for
gaps between the branches,
where slices of blue reach through.

I find myself mapping
those diminishing invitations of light,
gathering them up with my other options,
in case life gets too claustrophobic,
and I need an escape route.

Tornados

If you're from Oklahoma you
know the wind comes
sweeping down the
plain and the sky
turns night black
and the electric
air can be
tinted
green.
When the flashes startle
and the phantom miles
to the rumble diminish,
and the sirens curdle
your blood, you run
to huddle in the hall
closet believing the
frame is really a
shelter and all
your hot
breath
fills the
space
with
fear.
Tornados at a distance
pirouette drunkenly,
flirt with the ground.
like whips snapping,
stinging, touch down,
long greyish ropes
churning masonry
and memories
into match-
sticks and
dust.

Walking on the Pier at Calf Pasture Beach

The fisherman flung the sea robin off his line
onto the pier with a splat that hurt to hear.
It was a shimmering June afternoon
with summer rising between the toes
of the marsh grasses.

The sea robin, algae green with prickly fins,
lay gasping, drowning in oxygen,
surrounded by curious onlookers,
as the fisherman regaled them
about how its flesh continues to quiver,
even in the pan, even in the stomach.

From my bench looking out to the Norwalk islands,
I wanted to dive into the crowd, grab the dying fish,
release it back into the welcoming water,
to shout out that even this life deserves living.

But I am a coward.

Balcony Scene

The wasps flew crazed around the deck for days,
until the swift architecture of the spit-swirled,
clay-colored hive miraculously appeared.

One small sting, delivered just so,
could kill me, yet I cannot bear
to undo this hard-won castle.

I watch the wasps dance
in and out against the house,
sitting silently below them,
in the garden by the back steps,
unmoving, hypnotized,
courting danger
like a lover.

Front Yard Therapy

I am a frayed ribbon at the end of a satin day.

Dragonflies play tag through the lemon light
and the cool breath of sunset lifts my hair.

Barberry bushes with their prickly cowlicks
catch a spider crocheting a silver snood.

Ants march down the deck — a phalanx —
determined to conquer invisible crumbs.

Hummingbirds zoom to the feeder
for their five o'clock cocktail.
It's happy hour!

I only invite the evening in.

My worries close up for the night.

Bird Watching

Pigeons perch on the lampposts
wing to wing, rain or shine,
flutter off together in an arc,
loop de loop, return to their places,
feathered silhouettes in perfect order.

Where do they nest, what do they eat,
these gray onlookers high above the asphalt?

I like their camaraderie as they preen together,
and even the way they pretend to ignore
the red tail hawk two posts over
considering his options.

Phases of the Moon

The Moon is a communion wafer,
which feeds the earth a little heaven
while sprinkling diamond dust
across the world's night oceans.

The moon is a grandfather
with jovial, lined face,
who glows on his children
as they dance and play
by his silvery light.

The moon is a pirate ship
riding the cloudy seas,
a scythe to harvest stars,
a sphere for a cow
to jump over.

The moon is a backdrop
for departing geese at dusk,
foxes and wolves to howl against,
the silhouette of a kiss.

The moon is a guardian angel,
smiling in the window on cloudless nights,
caressing the graves where loved ones sleep
with iridescent fingers.

Visitation

The August night is so still,
my lamp shouts against the darkness,
and the old house doesn›t groan
without the wind.

As elusive as dark shadows
of mosquitoes flying against the light,
ideas try to fight their way from brain to pen,
but no translation tonight.

I slap a mosquito with my notebook,
just managing to kill it,
but another, as large as an angel, escapes,
making me itch in anticipation.

Weather Report

The angry afternoon subsides
leaving rain-spotted screens
and dripping, trees.
Heavy mountain air saunters in
with its mud, grass, and damp wood smell.
Alone on the porch,
a sudden line in my book
makes me think of you.

I have tried to find a place
for you in my life, and that failing,
I have tried to cram you in,
to fit where there is no fitting.

All you ever wanted to be
was a shadow, coming and going,
with all the irregularity of weather.

Walking at Dawn

The rosy sky reflected in the river
wears a thick gray hood,
and morning isn't promising anything.
I always hope for the best at six or seven,
when the thin line of light
dividing day and night
is uncommitted.

The robins and I,
the squirrels and mallards,
act like we own the place-
everybody chattering at once.
It's a moment of community,
with no strings attached.

Just in Case

I leave the bed on the right side,
reach for the face-up penny,
say rabbit on the first day of the month,
don't break the mirror, or step
on a crack.

I murmur bread and butter
to stave off separation,
eat blackeye peas on New Year's Day,
search for chimney sweeps,
knock on wood.

I keep a watch for rainbows,
gather four leaf clovers,
place "one to grow" on birthday cakes,
don't let a black cat
cross my path,

Eulogy for My Great Blue Heron

Out of the mirror of the dark and ominous pond,
at dusk in late November, beneath the Borglum Bridge,
a giant wing protrudes,
its feathered frame like an artist's installation,
the last remnant of a drowned blue heron.

I have seen him sunning on a boat in California
or fishing the mudflats around a pond in Georgia.
I have seen him resting in the trees along the Hudson,
swooping over the tide pools of Long Island Sound.
I am always on the lookout for his grey ghostly presence,
my lifter of spirits, talisman.

Entrapped in a tangle of abandoned fishing lines,
his squawks for help silenced, his struggle ended,
the exhausted blue curve of his neck
disappears under the dark water,
leaving one enormous, protesting wing,

Cape Cod — Autumn Revisit

The wet, fertile sea scent
of salt marsh and shellfish
is little changed since
the last time we were here,
twelve years and several deaths ago.

Streetlights spray the pewter veil
with a wash of white.
Halyards ping against their masts,
like bells ringing the hours.
Behind its grey scrim,
the cove is out there somewhere.

There is a hopeful forecast
for clear skies and Indian summer,
but hedges of beach plum,
queen Anne's lace, mud flats
with their broken shells and decaying life,
will only appear when the fog lifts,
one gossamer moment at a time.

Sanctuary

We leave the world for our weekly ritual,
don identical robes of moisture-proof nylon,
abandon ourselves to water.

We welcome the gentle laying on of hands,
which paints our faces green with medicinal mud,
twists our hair into Medusa locks,
and makes our eyebrows Romanesque arches.

Saints with halos of wired rollers, we meditate
under bubbles of glass and soporific air,
and breathe the familiar, restorative aromas
of hot wax and shampoos,
which drift in a gentle incense
amidst the incantation of female voices.

No fear or vanity here:
hair offered up in aluminum stalks.

Autumn Passage

Crimson and gold maple leaves
do their slow earthward dance,
leaving sad, bony branches.

The summer months left the room,
when I wasn't looking.

A ruby-throated hummingbird,
the last of our many regulars,
spends a final morning at the feeder,
tanking up for its miraculous flight south.

At night I hear crickets singing their fading litanies
about future hours of cold and dark,
while Time, the speed reader, turns the pages faster,
too eager to see how the story ends.

September 22 — Along the Hudson

The great blue heron crosses over Catskill Creek,
a shadow squawking into the marsh.

A group of pintails along the crowded dock
 preens and prepares for their yearly flight south.

The eagle on his high, forked branch
twists the white bulb of his head,
takes the oracles.

Slack tide and the creek is a silver mirror,
yachts, docks, and landscape stranded upside down.

A carillon from the Catholic Church
fills the air with Schubert's Ave Maria.

At the marina our boat *Swan Song*
perches on its trailer,
a For Sale sign catching the light.

New England October

Green algae icing over the pond,
hovering maples like dried out crones,
the silhouette of a great blue heron.

Chipmunks run around the rock walls,
as they collect and store seeds,
poke through the crickets' hedge of sound.

Autumn intoxication of fallen flower petals,
old leaves, a mash of summer ending.

I still love the whirl of October,
the overnight revelation of sky,
the animal sense of gathering in,
the solace of nature slowing down.

Naugatuck — November

In the Naugatuck valley, churches with peeling paint
stand with dignity alongside
the red brick hulks of former factories,
and Main Streets with their shabby shops.
For Rent signs exhale the odor of mildew,
infusing the air above uneven, cracked sidewalks.

On hills above the Naugatuck river,
once prosperous Victorian houses
with turrets and porticos
are carved into multiple apartments
behind mismatched curtains.

The glorious October leaves
are down and combed into orange piles.
Their dry, curled remnants rattle along the street
beneath the bruised November sky.

Glass Blower

Where are the blazing words
for the intensity of this fire,
which burns hard and blue?
I know neither its source
nor any purpose.

Goggled artisans
by their scalding furnaces
with their long pipes
blow liquid glass
into delicate shapes.

My fire just burns and waits
for the moment of inspiration,
        the flood of emotion,
                just the right word.

St. Mary's Cemetery — December 8, 1987

Above the still soft December earth,
family and friends hold each other up around the grave,
faces projecting from dark winter coats,
grief biting like frost.

Breath hangs white in the air like ghosts.

Draped over the bier's polished wood,
the flowers are already wilting.
Inside, David's hidden, diminishing weight
presses on his silk bedding.
Useless seeds inside him
prepare for their long sleep.

A yellow backhoe hides behind gaunt trees,
ready to bury the future.

Old Roses

I give you Moss and Damask roses:
ancient, romantic, fragrant,
with names evoking mystery,
queens and caravans
and history.

The petals are to bury your face in,
to press against your nose, your lips, your cheeks.
They bloom only once.
Hold them while you can.

I am a winter garden,
all thorns and frozen ground.

Still, I give you La Reine,
Maiden's Blush, Belle Amour —
this rich bouquet of roses.

Winter Vegetables

At the Morgan horse farm in Bloomfield,
where for room and board
I did the morning stable chores,
my landlady, Helen French, kept one acre
planted with vegetables for every season.

From asparagus to winter squash,
the kitchen fogged with huge pots,
boiling jars for the putting up
of produce for the frozen months.
Come January, reaching through the snow,
she pulled the pale parsnips
from their frosty mounds.

In the kitchen, I set the table
with its plastic, checkered cloth.
It squeezed against the wall
of faded paint and magazine clippings,
between stove and sink on cracked linoleum.

She told me tales of driving one-horse sleighs
the thirteen miles to Suffield
in the years when snow paved the ground
from December to March,
trotting through slumbering tobacco fields,
to supper at the Congregational Church
with its predictable offerings —
tomatoes, cucumbers, potatoes, beets,
pickled and canned, boiled and baked.

She flavored my imagination
with sugar, salt, and smoke,
all the while paring and steaming the parsnips,
setting them alongside the simmering stew,
pumpkin bread, strawberry jam, and succotash,
serving up a mid-winter banquet
from the nourishing goodness of the year.

Field Trip

The little child from the project
accompanies his kindergarten class
to see how maple syrup is being made.
But winter is late leaving
and the sap is frozen
in the silent trees.

The other children
in multicolored scarves and hats
run and jump in the cold.
The little child from the project shivers,
and snowflakes sit on his hair,
like white blossoms on black moss.

His teeth make a rhythmic clicking
and he lets me drape my muffler
around his head.
We pass a frozen pond
where ducks are huddled on the ice,
and he wonders aloud why they don't fly.

Together, we walk to the sugaring shed,
like modern magi, studying the sky.

Outside the Kitchen Window

The juncos scamper across the ice
like sandpipers on the beach
and kick up the snow,
as they stab the sunflower seeds
with their yellow sword beaks.
A dozen of them scatter into the fir tree —
black ornaments with alabaster bellies,
barely concealed by evergreen and bark.
They dance around the bird feeder,
joined by a pair of squirrels.
Acrobats in the wintry air, they flit and soar,
even on a day when another storm
makes the world an enormous snow globe.
Soon they'll sense the trend to warming air,
and waning mounds of cottony snow.
An invisible Pied Piper will lure them north
to their nests in the mountains of Canada,
with a promise of perpetually cool forests
and abundant forage,
and some March morning they'll disappear,
to frolic elsewhere until November,
when they'll come to play in our yard again.

Spinning

Branches glazed with rain,
embracing in the lamp light,
winter spider web.

Black X of spider,
silhouette against the snow,
frozen miracle.

Web of galaxies,
veiled by soft transparent mists,
silky breath of God.

Hot, shimmering bulb,
splaying out with golden rays,
sun with spider legs.

Ancient web of life,
twisted cords of yin and yang,
cradle of the world.

Golden Orb Spider

The black and golden spider waits,
nestled into the window track,
one of eight legs luxuriously extended.

Three floors up, outside our bedroom,
her large silver web sits suspended,
each section of its net precisely anchored
to a corner of the window frame.

When dusk begins to squeeze out the light,
she makes her way across the wires,
centers her body symmetrically on her filigree throne,
waits to see who's coming for dinner.

In bright lightning flashes
as late summer rains rage against the house,
she braves the storm to make repairs
on her tattered work of art.

I leave the curtains open, the lights on,
to aid her nightly hunting,
tape up a sign that says,
Do not open window!
Worry about the winter.

About the Author

Marsha Witham Whitman's career has been spent in music as teacher, choral conductor, arranger, translator, impresario, singer, and instrumentalist. A bachelor's and master's graduate of The Hartt School, she devoted over three decades to performing, teaching, and directing choirs, including pieces she commissioned. Since her childhood days moving around the US and Europe, she has kept a journal filled with both everyday experiences and poetry. These formative years contributed to a perpetual fascination with language, an abiding interest in nature, and a love of family history. Marsha lives in Connecticut where she raised a daughter and son with her husband Frank and now enjoys visiting them and her three grandchildren on both coasts.

www.ingramcontent.com/pod-product-compliance
Lightning Source LLC
Chambersburg PA
CBHW032025090426
42741CB00006B/734